This Book Belongs To

DATE: ___________________________________

MONTH: _______________   **SEASON:** _______________

TEMPERATURE: ___________________________________

COLOR IN THE PICTURES THAT DESCRIBE THE WEATHER TODAY

DRAW A PICTURE OF TODAY'S WEATHER

COLOR IN THE PICTURES THAT DESCRIBE THE WEATHER TODAY

DRAW A PICTURE OF TODAY'S WEATHER

DATE:

MONTH: SEASON:

TEMPERATURE:

COLOR IN THE PICTURES THAT DESCRIBE
THE WEATHER TODAY

DRAW A PICTURE OF TODAY'S WEATHER

DATE:

MONTH: SEASON:

TEMPERATURE:

COLOR IN THE PICTURES THAT DESCRIBE
THE WEATHER TODAY

DRAW A PICTURE OF TODAY'S WEATHER

DATE:

MONTH: **SEASON:**

TEMPERATURE:

COLOR IN THE PICTURES THAT DESCRIBE THE WEATHER TODAY

DRAW A PICTURE OF TODAY'S WEATHER

<u>DATE:</u>

<u>MONTH:</u>   <u>SEASON:</u>

<u>TEMPERATURE:</u>

COLOR IN THE PICTURES THAT DESCRIBE
THE WEATHER TODAY

DRAW A PICTURE OF TODAY'S WEATHER

DATE:

MONTH: **SEASON:**

TEMPERATURE:

COLOR IN THE PICTURES THAT DESCRIBE
THE WEATHER TODAY

DRAW A PICTURE OF TODAY'S WEATHER

<u>**DATE:**</u>

<u>**MONTH:**   **SEASON:**</u>

<u>**TEMPERATURE:**</u>

COLOR IN THE PICTURES THAT DESCRIBE THE WEATHER TODAY

DRAW A PICTURE OF TODAY'S WEATHER

DATE:

MONTH: **SEASON:**

TEMPERATURE:

COLOR IN THE PICTURES THAT DESCRIBE THE WEATHER TODAY

DRAW A PICTURE OF TODAY'S WEATHER

<u>**DATE:**</u>

<u>**MONTH:**   **SEASON:**</u>

<u>**TEMPERATURE:**</u>

COLOR IN THE PICTURES THAT DESCRIBE
THE WEATHER TODAY

DRAW A PICTURE OF TODAY'S WEATHER

DATE:

MONTH: **SEASON:**

TEMPERATURE:

COLOR IN THE PICTURES THAT DESCRIBE THE WEATHER TODAY

DRAW A PICTURE OF TODAY'S WEATHER

DATE:

MONTH: SEASON:

TEMPERATURE:

COLOR IN THE PICTURES THAT DESCRIBE
THE WEATHER TODAY

DRAW A PICTURE OF TODAY'S WEATHER

DATE:

MONTH: **SEASON:**

TEMPERATURE:

COLOR IN THE PICTURES THAT DESCRIBE THE WEATHER TODAY

DRAW A PICTURE OF TODAY'S WEATHER

COLOR IN THE PICTURES THAT DESCRIBE
THE WEATHER TODAY

DRAW A PICTURE OF TODAY'S WEATHER

DATE:

MONTH: SEASON:

TEMPERATURE:

COLOR IN THE PICTURES THAT DESCRIBE THE WEATHER TODAY

DRAW A PICTURE OF TODAY'S WEATHER

DATE:

MONTH: **SEASON:**

TEMPERATURE:

COLOR IN THE PICTURES THAT DESCRIBE THE WEATHER TODAY

DRAW A PICTURE OF TODAY'S WEATHER

DATE:

MONTH: SEASON:

TEMPERATURE:

COLOR IN THE PICTURES THAT DESCRIBE
THE WEATHER TODAY

DRAW A PICTURE OF TODAY'S WEATHER

DATE:

MONTH: SEASON:

TEMPERATURE:

COLOR IN THE PICTURES THAT DESCRIBE
THE WEATHER TODAY

DRAW A PICTURE OF TODAY'S WEATHER

DATE:

MONTH: **SEASON:**

TEMPERATURE:

COLOR IN THE PICTURES THAT DESCRIBE THE WEATHER TODAY

DRAW A PICTURE OF TODAY'S WEATHER

DATE:

MONTH: SEASON:

TEMPERATURE:

COLOR IN THE PICTURES THAT DESCRIBE
THE WEATHER TODAY

DRAW A PICTURE OF TODAY'S WEATHER

DATE:

MONTH: SEASON:

TEMPERATURE:

COLOR IN THE PICTURES THAT DESCRIBE THE WEATHER TODAY

DRAW A PICTURE OF TODAY'S WEATHER

DATE: _______________________________

MONTH: _______________ **SEASON:** _______________

TEMPERATURE: _______________________________

COLOR IN THE PICTURES THAT DESCRIBE THE WEATHER TODAY

DRAW A PICTURE OF TODAY'S WEATHER

DATE:

MONTH: SEASON:

TEMPERATURE:

COLOR IN THE PICTURES THAT DESCRIBE THE WEATHER TODAY

DRAW A PICTURE OF TODAY'S WEATHER

DATE:

MONTH: **SEASON:**

TEMPERATURE:

COLOR IN THE PICTURES THAT DESCRIBE THE WEATHER TODAY

DRAW A PICTURE OF TODAY'S WEATHER

DATE:

MONTH: SEASON:

TEMPERATURE:

COLOR IN THE PICTURES THAT DESCRIBE
THE WEATHER TODAY

DRAW A PICTURE OF TODAY'S WEATHER

DATE:

MONTH: **SEASON:**

TEMPERATURE:

COLOR IN THE PICTURES THAT DESCRIBE
THE WEATHER TODAY

DRAW A PICTURE OF TODAY'S WEATHER

DATE:

MONTH: SEASON:

TEMPERATURE:

COLOR IN THE PICTURES THAT DESCRIBE
THE WEATHER TODAY

DRAW A PICTURE OF TODAY'S WEATHER

DATE:

MONTH: **SEASON:**

TEMPERATURE:

COLOR IN THE PICTURES THAT DESCRIBE THE WEATHER TODAY

DRAW A PICTURE OF TODAY'S WEATHER

DATE:

MONTH: **SEASON:**

TEMPERATURE:

COLOR IN THE PICTURES THAT DESCRIBE THE WEATHER TODAY

DRAW A PICTURE OF TODAY'S WEATHER

<u>**DATE:**</u>

<u>**MONTH:**   **SEASON:**</u>

<u>**TEMPERATURE:**</u>

COLOR IN THE PICTURES THAT DESCRIBE
THE WEATHER TODAY

DRAW A PICTURE OF TODAY'S WEATHER

DATE:

____

MONTH: _____________ **SEASON:** _____________

TEMPERATURE: _____________

COLOR IN THE PICTURES THAT DESCRIBE
THE WEATHER TODAY

DRAW A PICTURE OF TODAY'S WEATHER

DATE:

MONTH: SEASON:

TEMPERATURE:

COLOR IN THE PICTURES THAT DESCRIBE THE WEATHER TODAY

DRAW A PICTURE OF TODAY'S WEATHER

DATE:

MONTH: SEASON:

TEMPERATURE:

COLOR IN THE PICTURES THAT DESCRIBE
THE WEATHER TODAY

DRAW A PICTURE OF TODAY'S WEATHER

COLOR IN THE PICTURES THAT DESCRIBE THE WEATHER TODAY

DRAW A PICTURE OF TODAY'S WEATHER

DATE:

MONTH: SEASON:

TEMPERATURE:

COLOR IN THE PICTURES THAT DESCRIBE THE WEATHER TODAY

DRAW A PICTURE OF TODAY'S WEATHER

DATE: ____

MONTH: _____________________ **SEASON:** _____________

TEMPERATURE: ____

COLOR IN THE PICTURES THAT DESCRIBE THE WEATHER TODAY

DRAW A PICTURE OF TODAY'S WEATHER

DATE:

MONTH: SEASON:

TEMPERATURE:

COLOR IN THE PICTURES THAT DESCRIBE THE WEATHER TODAY

DRAW A PICTURE OF TODAY'S WEATHER

DATE:

MONTH: SEASON:

TEMPERATURE:

COLOR IN THE PICTURES THAT DESCRIBE
THE WEATHER TODAY

DRAW A PICTURE OF TODAY'S WEATHER

COLOR IN THE PICTURES THAT DESCRIBE THE WEATHER TODAY

DRAW A PICTURE OF TODAY'S WEATHER

DATE:

MONTH: **SEASON:**

TEMPERATURE:

COLOR IN THE PICTURES THAT DESCRIBE THE WEATHER TODAY

DRAW A PICTURE OF TODAY'S WEATHER

DATE:

MONTH: SEASON:

TEMPERATURE:

COLOR IN THE PICTURES THAT DESCRIBE
THE WEATHER TODAY

DRAW A PICTURE OF TODAY'S WEATHER

DATE:

MONTH: SEASON:

TEMPERATURE:

COLOR IN THE PICTURES THAT DESCRIBE THE WEATHER TODAY

DRAW A PICTURE OF TODAY'S WEATHER

DATE:

MONTH: SEASON:

TEMPERATURE:

COLOR IN THE PICTURES THAT DESCRIBE
THE WEATHER TODAY

DRAW A PICTURE OF TODAY'S WEATHER

DATE:

MONTH: **SEASON:**

TEMPERATURE:

COLOR IN THE PICTURES THAT DESCRIBE THE WEATHER TODAY

DRAW A PICTURE OF TODAY'S WEATHER

<u>**DATE:**</u>

<u>**MONTH:**</u>   <u>**SEASON:**</u>

<u>**TEMPERATURE:**</u>

COLOR IN THE PICTURES THAT DESCRIBE THE WEATHER TODAY

DRAW A PICTURE OF TODAY'S WEATHER

DATE:

MONTH: SEASON:

TEMPERATURE:

COLOR IN THE PICTURES THAT DESCRIBE THE WEATHER TODAY

DRAW A PICTURE OF TODAY'S WEATHER

<u>**DATE:**</u>

<u>**MONTH:**</u>   **SEASON:**

<u>**TEMPERATURE:**</u>

COLOR IN THE PICTURES THAT DESCRIBE
THE WEATHER TODAY

DRAW A PICTURE OF TODAY'S WEATHER

DATE:

MONTH: **SEASON:**

TEMPERATURE:

COLOR IN THE PICTURES THAT DESCRIBE THE WEATHER TODAY

DRAW A PICTURE OF TODAY'S WEATHER

DATE:

MONTH: SEASON:

TEMPERATURE:

COLOR IN THE PICTURES THAT DESCRIBE THE WEATHER TODAY

DRAW A PICTURE OF TODAY'S WEATHER

DATE:

MONTH: SEASON:

TEMPERATURE:

COLOR IN THE PICTURES THAT DESCRIBE
THE WEATHER TODAY

DRAW A PICTURE OF TODAY'S WEATHER

DATE:

MONTH: **SEASON:**

TEMPERATURE:

COLOR IN THE PICTURES THAT DESCRIBE
THE WEATHER TODAY

DRAW A PICTURE OF TODAY'S WEATHER

DATE:

MONTH: **SEASON:**

TEMPERATURE:

COLOR IN THE PICTURES THAT DESCRIBE THE WEATHER TODAY

DRAW A PICTURE OF TODAY'S WEATHER

DATE:

MONTH: SEASON:

TEMPERATURE:

COLOR IN THE PICTURES THAT DESCRIBE
THE WEATHER TODAY

DRAW A PICTURE OF TODAY'S WEATHER

DATE:

MONTH: **SEASON:**

TEMPERATURE:

COLOR IN THE PICTURES THAT DESCRIBE THE WEATHER TODAY

DRAW A PICTURE OF TODAY'S WEATHER

DATE:

MONTH: **SEASON:**

TEMPERATURE:

COLOR IN THE PICTURES THAT DESCRIBE THE WEATHER TODAY

DRAW A PICTURE OF TODAY'S WEATHER

DATE:

MONTH: **SEASON:**

TEMPERATURE:

COLOR IN THE PICTURES THAT DESCRIBE
THE WEATHER TODAY

DRAW A PICTURE OF TODAY'S WEATHER

DATE:

MONTH: SEASON:

TEMPERATURE:

COLOR IN THE PICTURES THAT DESCRIBE THE WEATHER TODAY

DRAW A PICTURE OF TODAY'S WEATHER

DATE:

MONTH: ___________________ **SEASON:** ___________________

TEMPERATURE:

COLOR IN THE PICTURES THAT DESCRIBE THE WEATHER TODAY

DRAW A PICTURE OF TODAY'S WEATHER

DATE:

MONTH: SEASON:

TEMPERATURE:

COLOR IN THE PICTURES THAT DESCRIBE THE WEATHER TODAY

DRAW A PICTURE OF TODAY'S WEATHER

DATE:

MONTH: SEASON:

TEMPERATURE:

COLOR IN THE PICTURES THAT DESCRIBE
THE WEATHER TODAY

DRAW A PICTURE OF TODAY'S WEATHER

DATE:

MONTH: SEASON:

TEMPERATURE:

COLOR IN THE PICTURES THAT DESCRIBE THE WEATHER TODAY

DRAW A PICTURE OF TODAY'S WEATHER

DATE:

MONTH: SEASON:

TEMPERATURE:

COLOR IN THE PICTURES THAT DESCRIBE
THE WEATHER TODAY

DRAW A PICTURE OF TODAY'S WEATHER

<u>DATE:</u>

<u>MONTH:</u>   <u>SEASON:</u>

<u>TEMPERATURE:</u>

COLOR IN THE PICTURES THAT DESCRIBE THE WEATHER TODAY

DRAW A PICTURE OF TODAY'S WEATHER

DATE:

MONTH: **SEASON:**

TEMPERATURE:

COLOR IN THE PICTURES THAT DESCRIBE THE WEATHER TODAY

DRAW A PICTURE OF TODAY'S WEATHER

<u>**DATE:**</u>

<u>**MONTH:**</u>   <u>**SEASON:**</u>

<u>**TEMPERATURE:**</u>

COLOR IN THE PICTURES THAT DESCRIBE THE WEATHER TODAY

DRAW A PICTURE OF TODAY'S WEATHER

DATE:

MONTH: **SEASON:**

TEMPERATURE:

COLOR IN THE PICTURES THAT DESCRIBE THE WEATHER TODAY

DRAW A PICTURE OF TODAY'S WEATHER

DATE:

MONTH: SEASON:

TEMPERATURE:

COLOR IN THE PICTURES THAT DESCRIBE
THE WEATHER TODAY

DRAW A PICTURE OF TODAY'S WEATHER

DATE: _______________________________

MONTH: _____________ **SEASON:** _____________

TEMPERATURE: _______________________________

COLOR IN THE PICTURES THAT DESCRIBE
THE WEATHER TODAY

DRAW A PICTURE OF TODAY'S WEATHER

DATE:

MONTH: SEASON:

TEMPERATURE:

COLOR IN THE PICTURES THAT DESCRIBE
THE WEATHER TODAY

DRAW A PICTURE OF TODAY'S WEATHER

DATE:

MONTH: **SEASON:**

TEMPERATURE:

COLOR IN THE PICTURES THAT DESCRIBE THE WEATHER TODAY

DRAW A PICTURE OF TODAY'S WEATHER

DATE:

MONTH: **SEASON:**

TEMPERATURE:

COLOR IN THE PICTURES THAT DESCRIBE THE WEATHER TODAY

DRAW A PICTURE OF TODAY'S WEATHER

DATE:

MONTH: SEASON:

TEMPERATURE:

COLOR IN THE PICTURES THAT DESCRIBE THE WEATHER TODAY

DRAW A PICTURE OF TODAY'S WEATHER

DATE:

MONTH: SEASON:

TEMPERATURE:

COLOR IN THE PICTURES THAT DESCRIBE
THE WEATHER TODAY

DRAW A PICTURE OF TODAY'S WEATHER

COLOR IN THE PICTURES THAT DESCRIBE
THE WEATHER TODAY

DRAW A PICTURE OF TODAY'S WEATHER

DATE:

MONTH: SEASON:

TEMPERATURE:

COLOR IN THE PICTURES THAT DESCRIBE
THE WEATHER TODAY

DRAW A PICTURE OF TODAY'S WEATHER

DATE:

MONTH: SEASON:

TEMPERATURE:

COLOR IN THE PICTURES THAT DESCRIBE THE WEATHER TODAY

DRAW A PICTURE OF TODAY'S WEATHER

DATE:

MONTH: **SEASON:**

TEMPERATURE:

COLOR IN THE PICTURES THAT DESCRIBE THE WEATHER TODAY

DRAW A PICTURE OF TODAY'S WEATHER

DATE:

MONTH: **SEASON:**

TEMPERATURE:

COLOR IN THE PICTURES THAT DESCRIBE
THE WEATHER TODAY

DRAW A PICTURE OF TODAY'S WEATHER

DATE:

MONTH: **SEASON:**

TEMPERATURE:

COLOR IN THE PICTURES THAT DESCRIBE THE WEATHER TODAY

DRAW A PICTURE OF TODAY'S WEATHER

DATE:

MONTH: SEASON:

TEMPERATURE:

COLOR IN THE PICTURES THAT DESCRIBE
THE WEATHER TODAY

DRAW A PICTURE OF TODAY'S WEATHER

DATE:

MONTH: SEASON:

TEMPERATURE:

COLOR IN THE PICTURES THAT DESCRIBE
THE WEATHER TODAY

DRAW A PICTURE OF TODAY'S WEATHER

DATE:

MONTH: **SEASON:**

TEMPERATURE:

COLOR IN THE PICTURES THAT DESCRIBE
THE WEATHER TODAY

DRAW A PICTURE OF TODAY'S WEATHER

DATE:

MONTH: SEASON:

TEMPERATURE:

COLOR IN THE PICTURES THAT DESCRIBE
THE WEATHER TODAY

DRAW A PICTURE OF TODAY'S WEATHER

<u>DATE:</u>

<u>MONTH:</u>   <u>SEASON:</u>

<u>TEMPERATURE:</u>

COLOR IN THE PICTURES THAT DESCRIBE THE WEATHER TODAY

DRAW A PICTURE OF TODAY'S WEATHER

DATE:

MONTH: **SEASON:**

TEMPERATURE:

COLOR IN THE PICTURES THAT DESCRIBE
THE WEATHER TODAY

DRAW A PICTURE OF TODAY'S WEATHER

DATE:

MONTH: SEASON:

TEMPERATURE:

COLOR IN THE PICTURES THAT DESCRIBE
THE WEATHER TODAY

DRAW A PICTURE OF TODAY'S WEATHER

<u>DATE:</u>

<u>MONTH:</u>   <u>SEASON:</u>

<u>TEMPERATURE:</u>

COLOR IN THE PICTURES THAT DESCRIBE THE WEATHER TODAY

DRAW A PICTURE OF TODAY'S WEATHER

DATE: ____

MONTH: _______________ **SEASON:** _______________

TEMPERATURE: _____________________________________

COLOR IN THE PICTURES THAT DESCRIBE
THE WEATHER TODAY

DRAW A PICTURE OF TODAY'S WEATHER

DATE:

MONTH: SEASON:

TEMPERATURE:

COLOR IN THE PICTURES THAT DESCRIBE THE WEATHER TODAY

DRAW A PICTURE OF TODAY'S WEATHER

COLOR IN THE PICTURES THAT DESCRIBE
THE WEATHER TODAY

DRAW A PICTURE OF TODAY'S WEATHER

DATE:

MONTH: SEASON:

TEMPERATURE:

COLOR IN THE PICTURES THAT DESCRIBE THE WEATHER TODAY

DRAW A PICTURE OF TODAY'S WEATHER

DATE: ____

MONTH: ___________ **SEASON:** ___________

TEMPERATURE: ___________________________________

COLOR IN THE PICTURES THAT DESCRIBE
THE WEATHER TODAY

DRAW A PICTURE OF TODAY'S WEATHER

DATE:

MONTH: SEASON:

TEMPERATURE:

COLOR IN THE PICTURES THAT DESCRIBE
THE WEATHER TODAY

DRAW A PICTURE OF TODAY'S WEATHER

DATE:

MONTH: SEASON:

TEMPERATURE:

COLOR IN THE PICTURES THAT DESCRIBE
THE WEATHER TODAY

DRAW A PICTURE OF TODAY'S WEATHER

DATE:

MONTH: **SEASON:**

TEMPERATURE:

COLOR IN THE PICTURES THAT DESCRIBE THE WEATHER TODAY

DRAW A PICTURE OF TODAY'S WEATHER

DATE: ______________________________

MONTH: ______________   **SEASON:** ______________

TEMPERATURE: ______________________________

COLOR IN THE PICTURES THAT DESCRIBE THE WEATHER TODAY

DRAW A PICTURE OF TODAY'S WEATHER

DATE:

MONTH: **SEASON:**

TEMPERATURE:

COLOR IN THE PICTURES THAT DESCRIBE THE WEATHER TODAY

DRAW A PICTURE OF TODAY'S WEATHER

DATE:

MONTH: **SEASON:**

TEMPERATURE:

COLOR IN THE PICTURES THAT DESCRIBE
THE WEATHER TODAY

DRAW A PICTURE OF TODAY'S WEATHER

DATE:

MONTH: SEASON:

TEMPERATURE:

COLOR IN THE PICTURES THAT DESCRIBE THE WEATHER TODAY

DRAW A PICTURE OF TODAY'S WEATHER

DATE:

MONTH: SEASON:

TEMPERATURE:

COLOR IN THE PICTURES THAT DESCRIBE THE WEATHER TODAY

DRAW A PICTURE OF TODAY'S WEATHER

DATE:

MONTH: SEASON:

TEMPERATURE:

COLOR IN THE PICTURES THAT DESCRIBE THE WEATHER TODAY

DRAW A PICTURE OF TODAY'S WEATHER

DATE:

MONTH: SEASON:

TEMPERATURE:

COLOR IN THE PICTURES THAT DESCRIBE THE WEATHER TODAY

DRAW A PICTURE OF TODAY'S WEATHER

DATE:

MONTH: SEASON:

TEMPERATURE:

COLOR IN THE PICTURES THAT DESCRIBE THE WEATHER TODAY

DRAW A PICTURE OF TODAY'S WEATHER

COLOR IN THE PICTURES THAT DESCRIBE
THE WEATHER TODAY

DRAW A PICTURE OF TODAY'S WEATHER

DATE:

MONTH: SEASON:

TEMPERATURE:

COLOR IN THE PICTURES THAT DESCRIBE THE WEATHER TODAY

DRAW A PICTURE OF TODAY'S WEATHER

DATE:

MONTH: ___________________ **SEASON:**

TEMPERATURE:

COLOR IN THE PICTURES THAT DESCRIBE
THE WEATHER TODAY

DRAW A PICTURE OF TODAY'S WEATHER

DATE:

MONTH: **SEASON:**

TEMPERATURE:

COLOR IN THE PICTURES THAT DESCRIBE
THE WEATHER TODAY

DRAW A PICTURE OF TODAY'S WEATHER

COLOR IN THE PICTURES THAT DESCRIBE THE WEATHER TODAY

DRAW A PICTURE OF TODAY'S WEATHER

DATE:

MONTH: **SEASON:**

TEMPERATURE:

COLOR IN THE PICTURES THAT DESCRIBE
THE WEATHER TODAY

DRAW A PICTURE OF TODAY'S WEATHER

DATE:

MONTH: SEASON:

TEMPERATURE:

COLOR IN THE PICTURES THAT DESCRIBE
THE WEATHER TODAY

DRAW A PICTURE OF TODAY'S WEATHER

DATE:

MONTH: **SEASON:**

TEMPERATURE:

COLOR IN THE PICTURES THAT DESCRIBE THE WEATHER TODAY

DRAW A PICTURE OF TODAY'S WEATHER

DATE:

MONTH: SEASON:

TEMPERATURE:

COLOR IN THE PICTURES THAT DESCRIBE THE WEATHER TODAY

DRAW A PICTURE OF TODAY'S WEATHER

DATE:

MONTH: SEASON:

TEMPERATURE:

COLOR IN THE PICTURES THAT DESCRIBE
THE WEATHER TODAY

DRAW A PICTURE OF TODAY'S WEATHER

COLOR IN THE PICTURES THAT DESCRIBE
THE WEATHER TODAY

DRAW A PICTURE OF TODAY'S WEATHER

DATE:

MONTH: SEASON:

TEMPERATURE:

COLOR IN THE PICTURES THAT DESCRIBE THE WEATHER TODAY

DRAW A PICTURE OF TODAY'S WEATHER

<u>**DATE:**</u>

<u>**MONTH:**</u>　　　　　　**SEASON:**

<u>**TEMPERATURE:**</u>

COLOR IN THE PICTURES THAT DESCRIBE
THE WEATHER TODAY

DRAW A PICTURE OF TODAY'S WEATHER

<u>**DATE:**</u>

<u>**MONTH:**</u>　　　　　　　　　　<u>**SEASON:**</u>

<u>**TEMPERATURE:**</u>

COLOR IN THE PICTURES THAT DESCRIBE THE WEATHER TODAY

DRAW A PICTURE OF TODAY'S WEATHER

DATE:

MONTH: SEASON:

TEMPERATURE:

COLOR IN THE PICTURES THAT DESCRIBE
THE WEATHER TODAY

DRAW A PICTURE OF TODAY'S WEATHER

DATE:

MONTH: **SEASON:**

TEMPERATURE:

COLOR IN THE PICTURES THAT DESCRIBE
THE WEATHER TODAY

DRAW A PICTURE OF TODAY'S WEATHER